WORLD FAMOUS QUICHE

Quick and Delicious Quiche Cookbook

Lara Bennet

Copyright © 2015

Readers shall not transmit or reproduce any part of this book in any form including print, electronic, photocopying, scanning, mechanical, or recording without prior written permission from the author.

While the author has taken utmost efforts to ensure the accuracy of the written content, it is advisable for all readers to follow the information mentioned herein at their own risk. The author is not responsible for any personal or commercial damage caused by misinterpretation of information.

CONTENTS

World Famous Quiche Recipes 1
   Conversion Table 5
   Abbreviations 5
   Introduction to Quiche 6
   Tomato Quiche 7
   Rainbow Quiche 8
   Ham 'n' Cheese Quiche 10
   Mushroom Asparagus Quiche 11
   Bacon Vegetable Quiche 13
   Ham and Swiss Quiche 14
   Butternut Squash and Bacon Quiche 16
   Shallot-Mushroom Quiche 17
   Broccoli-Cheddar Quiche 18
   Spinach Swiss Quiche 19
   Bacon-Cheese Quiche 20
   Pepperoni Spinach Quiche 22
   Potato Crust Quiche 23
   Bacon Swiss Quiche Recipe 24
   Cheesy Zucchini Quiche 25
   Asparagus Custard Tart 27
   Ham-and-Potato Bake 29
   Swiss Chard, Mushroom, and White-Cheddar Quiche 30
   Caramelized Garlic Tart 32
   Asparagus, Leek, and Gruyere Quiche 34
   Sausage-Potato Quiche 35

Thank You 37

CONVERSION TABLE

- 1/2 fl oz = 3 tsp = 1 tbsp = 15 ml
- 1 fl oz = 2 tbsp = 1/8c = 30 ml
- 2 fl oz = 4 tbsp = 3/4c = 60 ml
- 4 fl oz = 8 tbsp = 1/2c = 118 ml
- 8 fl oz = 16 tbsp = 1c = 236 ml
- 16 fl oz = 1 pt = 1/2 qt = 2 c = 473 ml
- 128 fl oz = 8 pt = 4 qt = 1 gal = 3.78 L

ABBREVIATIONS

- oz = ounce
- fl oz = fluid ounce
- tsp = teaspoon
- tbsp = tablespoon
- ml = milliliter
- c = cup
- pt = pint
- qt = quart
- gal = gallon
- L = liter

INTRODUCTION TO QUICHE

Quiche is a spicy open pastry crust with mouthwatering custard-cheese filling, which also has vegetables or meat and seafood. Quiche are good to serve chilled or hot, anyway you like it. This egg-crusted dish is a traditional brunch and a favorite for many.

Making it is quite easy too, and the savory ingredients can vary from Gruyere or Swiss cheese to other modern additions.

Some people say that the origins of this recipe go back to France, and it does seem quite accurate because in its original form, it has attributes of French taste and style. However, it is a fact that before the French concocted the Quiche, German chefs started making an egg-custard pie, named Kuchen, which means "cake."

The German chefs baked Kuchen in brioche dough and not the typical piecrust. They added egg and cream to bacon and then baked it in the brioche shell.

There is still a lot of confusion among food historians about which of the two (Germans or French) began the idea of using pastry shell, but its ingredients included of flour, butter or lard, and cold water. However, the French get credit for the most popular form – the Quiche Lorraine. This at first only comprised of bacon. Adding cheese came much later.

It wasn't until 1950s that Quiche began to gain popularity in England. The English began making variants of the Quiche recipe using egg pie and ham with a top crust. English men began to avoid the dish because its main ingredients were vegetables, which gave rise to the concept of its not being the ideal dish for "real men."

In the present times, Julia Child gets credit in the U.S. for introducing Quiche to modern day recipes. In many homes, her recipe books that comprised mostly of French recipes became staples. There are some modifications in her recipes though, for instance she forgoes bacon in Quiche Lorraine, and replaces it with extra cheese.

In 1970, serving Quiche became a classic treat and part of dinner and brunch in many homes and occasions.

The most challenging part of cooking quiche is making sure that the filling doesn't leak out of the piecrust. The crust has to be only bake partially, and to prevent it from rising too much, you have to mark it with fork. By marking sure it doesn't rise, you make sure that the contents remain inside. If they leak, it will ruin the delight of mystery of the dish.

Today, new chefs continue to develop new ideas about how to bake the pie shell, using an additional aluminum pie dish on top, and using dry beans to weigh it down. They use virtually anything that can provide just enough weight.

Beans are an affordable way to prevent rising of the crust, so cooks use it more often, although rice and dried peas also work very well. Another successful trick is brushing egg white on the partially baked shell to reduce leakage.

Quiche is not a low-fat dish, because most of the pastry crust comprises of large amounts of saturated fats. Some additions can reduce the calorie, like using milk instead of cream. Alternatively, you can use reduced fat cheese instead of higher fat cheese.

The best part about this dish is that even with modifications to control the overall fat content; the rich taste rewards the pallets.

TOMATO QUICHE

This is the most requested recipe at family parties, lunches, and dinner. It is very appetizing for everyone during summer, and you can serve it cold or hot. Everyone loves it! Making it is a fun experience and extremely easy.

Ingredients:

- 1/4 teaspoon pepper
- 1/4 teaspoon dried thyme

- 1 teaspoon salt
- 1 unbaked pastry shell
- 1 cup chopped onion
- 1-1/2 cups half-and-half cream
- 2 tablespoons butter
- 2 cups Monterey Jack cheese, divided
- 4 eggs
- 4 large tomatoes, peeled, seeded, chopped and drained

Directions:

1. Sauté the onions in butter using a large skillet; then add pepper, salt, and thyme with the tomatoes. Cook this mixture over medium heat until the onions and tomatoes leave water and it evaporates until it almost dries. This could take about 10-15 minutes. After that, remove the skillet from the flame.
2. Add 1 cup of the cheese into the pie shell, at the bottom. Cover it with a layer of the tomato mix and sprinkle the remaining cheese on it.
3. Beat the eggs in a small bowl until the mixture turns foamy, and then beat in the cream. Once smooth, pour it into the pie shell.
4. Put in a preheated oven at 425^0 and bake for 10 minutes. You can reduce the heat to 325^0 and bake for an additional 40 minutes until it turns brown. Use a knife and insert it in the center to see if it comes out clean. Once baked, let it stand for at least ten minutes before cutting. This recipe yields 6-8 servings.

RAINBOW QUICHE

If you want Quiche with lots of creamy-egg cheese filling and veggies, then the Rainbow Quiche is going to be your favorite recipe.

Ingredients:

- 1/2 teaspoon salt
- 2 tablespoons butter
- 1-1/2 cups chopped broccoli florets
- 1 each small green, sweet red and orange peppers, chopped
- 1 small onion, finely chopped
- 1 cup chopped fresh spinach
- 1 cup sliced fresh mushrooms
- 1 cup shredded Mexican cheese blend
- 1-3/4 cups 2% milk
- 6 large eggs, lightly beaten
- Pastry for single-crust pie

Directions:

1. First, preheat the oven at 350^0. While it heats, line a 9-inch deep pie plate with the pastry, trim the edges and flute them. Sauté the onions, peppers, mushrooms, and broccoli in butter until almost cooked and tender. Add the spinach also. Spoon this mixture into the crust you've prepared and sprinkle some cheese. Whisk the eggs with milk, and add salt to it and pour this over the cheese.
2. Let it bake for 45-55 minutes or until you insert the knife and it comes out clean. Once baked, let it stand for at least ten minutes before you cut it.
3. If you choose to freeze it, wrap individual portions of the cooled Quiche in plastic wraps or foil paper and then freeze. When you want to use it, partially thaw it

by keeping it in the refrigerator overnight. To bake it, remove it from the refrigerator at least 30 minutes before you bake it.
4. Preheat the oven at 350^0, unwrap it, and then bake it. Place a thermometer in the center and make sure it reads a temperature of 165^0. It serves 8.

HAM 'N' CHEESE QUICHE

This is the perfect recipe to store and use later. Let's say, if you need to freeze something and serve it instantly whenever the need arises, then Ham 'n' cheese quiche can be the best recipe.

For some couples who were having a baby, freezing these was a great idea because when they were too tired after the birth of their new family member, this readymade meal was very handy and a relief for both.

You can easily make it and freeze it too.

Ingredients:

- 1/4 teaspoon pepper
- 1/2 teaspoon salt
- 1 package refrigerated pie pastry
- 2 teaspoons dried minced onion
- 2 cups diced fully cooked ham
- 2 cups half-and-half cream
- 2 cups shredded sharp cheddar cheese
- 4 eggs

Directions:

1. While you preheat the oven at 400^0, prepare two 9-inch pastry sheets by unrolling them into pie plates with flute edges. With a heavy-duty foil of double

thickness, line the un-pricked pastry shells. Fill in the dried beans or uncooked rice to add weight and bake it for 10-12 minutes (until it turns light golden brown). Then remove the weights and foil, and bake for an additional 3-5 minutes or maybe longer until it turns golden brown. Remove it and place it on cooling racks.
2. Separate portions of the cheese, onions, and ham between the shells. Then whisk eggs with some cream, pepper, and salt in a large bowl and make sure it blends well. Then pour this into the shells. Cover the edges with foil, but keep it lose. Bake it for 34-40 minutes, or until you feel sure that if you insert a knife into the center, it will come out clean. Then let it stand for 5-10 minutes and then cut it.
3. If you want to freeze it, cover it and freeze it while it is unbaked. To bake it, remove it from the freezer at least 30 minutes earlier, but do not thaw it. Preheat the oven at 350^0 and then put the Quiche on the baking sheet. Use foil to cover the edges loosely and bake as directed above. Use a knife to check if it is cooked.

This recipe will yield two Quiches, which serves six people easily.

MUSHROOM ASPARAGUS QUICHE

In this recipe, you need to use many asparagus. They add flavor and color to the Quiche, making it creamy too. The easy crescent roll crust means that you will have dinner ready in an impulse.

Ingredients:

- 1/4 teaspoon each dried basil, oregano and rubbed sage

- 1/4 teaspoon garlic powder
- 1/2 teaspoon pepper
- 1/2 teaspoon salt
- 1 tube refrigerated crescent rolls
- 1 medium onion, chopped
- 2 cups shredded part-skim mozzarella cheese
- 2 teaspoons prepared mustard
- 2 eggs, lightly beaten
- 1-1/2 pounds fresh asparagus, trimmed and cut into 1/2-inch pieces
- 1/2 cup sliced fresh mushrooms
- 1/4 cup minced fresh parsley
- 1/4 cup butter, cubed

Directions:

1. After preparing the crest dough, separate it into eight triangles. Place them into an ungreased 9-inch pie plate, keeping the points towards the center. Press it at the bottom and along the sides to make the crust. Spread some mustard, and keep this aside.
2. Sauté the asparagus, mushrooms, and onions, in a large skillet with some butter until the asparagus turn crisp and tender. Then combine the remaining ingredients in the asparagus mixture and pour them into the crust.
3. Put the pie pan into the oven, and bake it at 375o for twenty-five to thirsty minutes. You can check if it's ready by inserting a knife near the center and see if it comes out clean. Once baked, let it stand for at least ten minutes before you cut it into eight pieces. It serves eight people easily.
4. If you find my recipe valuable, please a couple of minutes to rate my book. I'll be eternally grateful if

you leave a review. I rely on reviews from my readers because I am an independent author, and I find great pleasure in seeing my work appreciated.

BACON VEGETABLE QUICHE

If you are looking for a nifty recipe, then you will love making bacon vegetable Quiche. You have the option to use leeks, Vidalia onions, or green onions. To replace the broccoli, you can use asparagus and any other herbs, or even cheese. You will love this Quiche recipe particularly during spring.

Ingredients:

- 1/4 teaspoon pepper
- 1/4 teaspoon salt
- 1/2 cup crumbled tomato and basil feta cheese
- 1 tablespoon minced fresh rosemary or 1 teaspoon dried rosemary, crushed
- 3/4 cup chopped sweet onion
- 1 can (5 ounces) evaporated milk
- 1 cup shredded cheddar cheese
- 1 unbaked pastry shell
- 1 cup chopped fresh broccoli
- 1 cup sliced fresh mushrooms
- 2-1/2 teaspoons olive oil
- 2 cups fresh baby spinach
- 3 large eggs, lightly beaten
- 6 bacon strips, cooked and crumbled

Directions:

1. Preheat the oven at 450°. Using a double thickness heavy-duty foil, line the un-pricked pastry shell and let it bake for 8 minutes. When done, remove the foil

and bake it for another 5 minutes. Reduce the heat of the oven to 375°.
2. While it bakes, sauté the mushrooms with broccoli and onion in oil until tender in a large skillet. At the end, add spinach and cook it until wilted.
3. Take a bowl and whisk eggs with some milk and rosemary. Add in the bacon, vegetables, and cheddar cheese. Add salt and pepper to your taste. Once ready, pour this into the crust and sprinkle the feta cheese.
4. Make sure you cover the edges with foil, but keep it loose. Let it bake for 30-35 minutes or until you insert the knife and it comes out clean. Do not cut it immediately; let it stand for five minutes.
5. If you prefer to freeze it until later, freeze it in the unfrozen form and keep it covered securely. To use it, remove it from the freezer at least 30 minutes before you bake. Do not let it thaw. Let the oven preheat to 375^0 and then place the Quiche on a baking sheet. Make sure you cove the edges loosely using foil. You can increase the time if necessary until the knife comes out clean when you insert it in the center. This recipe serves 6 people.

HAM AND SWISS QUICHE

This is a tender piecrust recipe with savory filling that even people who need gluten-free recipes can enjoy. It is a classic ham-and-cheese Quiche recipe with easy-to-knead dough. Since it is gluten free, you don't have to worry about its becoming too tough with kneading.

Ingredients:

- 1/3 cup whole milk
- 1/2 cup shredded Swiss

- 1 teaspoon fresh thyme leaves
- 1 recipe Gluten-Free Pie Dough
- 1 large yellow onion, halved and thinly sliced
- 2 teaspoons olive oil
- 4 ounces ham steak, cut into small cubes (about 1 cup)
- 5 large eggs plus 2 large egg whites
- Gluten-free all-purpose flour, for rolling
- Coarse salt and pepper

Directions:

1. Preheat the oven at 400^0 but place the rack in the upper and lower thirds of the oven. Toss the onion, thyme, and oil on a rimmed baking sheet and spread evenly into a single layer. Season it with pepper and salt.
2. On a floured surface roll out the dough into a 12-inch circle using a rolling pin. Transfer this to a 9-inch pie plate, and fold the overhangs under the tray and crimp the edges. If the dough cracks, use the extra dough to patch it. Use parchment sheet and fill the pie weights or dried beans. Place the onion on the top rack and the dough on the bottom rack and bake until the onion is soft and the crust appears dried on the edges and light golden. Let it bake for 15-18 minutes and then remove the parchment sheet and weights.
3. In a medium size bowl, whisk the egg whites and eggs, milk, ¼ tsp pepper and ½ tsp salt. Mix in the ham, onions, and shredded Swiss. Pour this into the crust, place it on the top rack of the oven, and bake it for 25 minutes, until the center is set. Serve it while warm or at room temperature.

BUTTERNUT SQUASH AND BACON QUICHE

If you want a firm and crispy Quiche recipe, then you must try this one. Try our Flaky Pie Dough and prebake the tart shell. Serve this Quiche recipe for brunch, lunch, or dinner.

Ingredients:

- 1 recipe Flaky Pie Dough or store-bought
- 1 medium yellow onion, halved and thinly sliced
- 3/4 pound butternut squash, peeled, halved, and very thinly sliced
- 1/2 cup heavy cream
- 1/2 cup whole milk
- 6 fresh sage leaves
- 8 large eggs
- 8 slices bacon
- All-purpose flour, for rolling dough
- Coarse salt and ground pepper

Directions:

1. Preheat the oven at 350^0. Roll out the dough on a floured surface into an 11-to-15 inch rectangle. Transfer it to a 9-13 inch baking pan. Fold the edges of the dough in a way to make the sides 1 inch high. Use a fork to prick the dough and put it into the freezer for 15 minutes until it becomes firm.
2. Press the parchment paper or foil over the dough and let it drape over the rim of the pan. Place the pie weight over the dough and bake until golden and dry. This may take 10 minutes.
3. While the crust bakes, cook the bacon in a large skillet until crisp, over medium flame for 10 minutes. Flip it over just once. Drain off the oil using paper towels. Add onions to the skillet and season it with pepper

and salt. Stir often while cooking until golden brown (or for 10 minutes). Spread this mixture in the crust evenly and top it with squash. Overlap the slices and add a piece of bacon in every few rows.
4. Whisk the milk, egg, and cream together in a bowl, and season it with pepper and salt. Pour enough of the egg mixture to fill the top of the crust. Also, use sage in the topping. Let it bake until the center has set and the edges puff up. This may take 45 minutes. Let it cool for 15 minutes before cutting and serving.

SHALLOT-MUSHROOM QUICHE

This is a versatile recipe, which you can serve for brunch or dinner. It goes very well with leafy green salad. Its flaky crust filled with custard makes it a perfect recipe to explore new options. In this recipe also, you have to use the blind-baking technique to keep it soggy.

Ingredients:

- 3/4 pound mushrooms, thinly sliced and sautéed
- 3/4 cup heavy cream
- 1 tablespoon unsalted butter
- 1 homemade or store-bought single-crust pie dough
- 1 cup grated fontina
- 2 cups thinly sliced shallots
- 6 large eggs
- All-purpose flour, for rolling dough
- Coarse salt and ground pepper

Directions:

1. First, preheat the oven at 374^0. While it heats, roll the dough using a rolling pin into a 12-inch circle. Put

this into a 9-inch pie plate, and fold the overhanging under the edges and crimp them. Use parchment paper and weights over the dough. Bake it for 20 minutes until it turns light golden and brown.
2. In the meanwhile, melt butter in a large skillet over medium flame. Add in the shallots and season with pepper and salt. Cook it until golden for 8-10 minutes.
3. In a medium size bowl, whisk the eggs and cream together. Add the shallots with mushrooms and cheese. Season this with ½ tsp salt and ¼ tsp pepper. Whisk the mixture and pour it into the crust. Bake it until the center is firm for 40-45 minutes. Use a knife to check. Serve it warm or cool it to room temperature before serving.

BROCCOLI-CHEDDAR QUICHE

This dish is an amazing recipe for every occasion. You can serve it for a brunch buffet or at a dinner party. Its crust stays flaky even when filled with custard. It also uses the blind-baking technique to prevent it from becoming soggy.

Ingredients:

- 3/4 pound broccoli florets, steamed until crisp-tender
- 3/4 cup heavy cream
- 1 tablespoon unsalted butter
- 1 cup grated sharp cheddar
- 1 homemade or store-bought single-crust pie dough
- 2 cups medium diced yellow onion
- 6 large eggs
- Coarse salt and ground pepper
- All-purpose flour, for rolling dough

Directions:

1. You must preheat the oven at 375^0. Roll out the dough to a 12-inch circle and place it in a 9-inch pie plate. Use parchment and dried bean seeds to add weight on top of the dough and then bake it until golden brown or use a knife to check the center. This may take 20 minutes. Then remove the parchment and weight.
2. In the meantime, sauté the onion in melted butter over medium heat. Cook for 8-10 minutes, and season with pepper and salt.
3. Whisk some eggs with the cream, in a medium bowl. Toss in the broccoli florets, onions, and cheese. Season it with ¼ tsp pepper and ½ tsp salt. Whisk it to mix well, then pour it into the crust and bake it for 40-45 minutes until the crust turns golden. Serve it warm, or cool it at room temperature.

SPINACH SWISS QUICHE

This mouthwatering Quiche recipe has wedges filled with sweet red pepper, frozen spinach, and creamy Swiss cheese. This recipe works for all occasions throughout the year. If you want to add some bacon to it, then sauté it a night before the day you want to bake it, to save time.

Ingredients:

- 1/4 cup chopped sweet red pepper
- 1/4 teaspoon each salt, pepper and paprika
- 1/4 teaspoon dried parsley flakes
- 1/4 cup chopped onion
- 1/4 cup shredded reduced-fat Swiss cheese
- 1/2 teaspoon dried oregano

- 1/2 cup fat-free cottage cheese
- 1 package (about 10 ounces) frozen chopped spinach, thawed and squeezed dry
- 1 refrigerated pie pastry
- 2 cups egg substitute
- 4 turkey bacon strips, diced
- 6 tablespoons fat-free sour cream

Directions:

1. Roll out the pastry on a floured surface. Then transfer it to a 9-inch pie plate. Trim it to ½ inch from the edge and flute the edges. Line the un-pricked pastry using heavy duty foil with double thickness
2. Preheat the oven and bake at 450^0 for about 8 minutes. Then bake for 5 minutes extra just to make sure it bakes. Take it out and place it on a wire rack to cool. In the meantime, reduce the heat of the oven to 350^0.
3. Cook the bacon in a small skillet, add red pepper and the onions, and cook until tender. Add in the spinach and then put a spoonful of the mixture into the pastry.
4. Combine egg substitute, Swiss cheese, cottage cheese and the seasoning and pour this over the spinach mixture. Serve hot.

BACON-CHEESE QUICHE

This recipe is ideal for those who want to serve a snappy meal with leafy green salads. It has a flaky crust with custard filling that makes it a perfect brunch or dinner recipe. The tricky part of this recipe is that you have to 'blind bake' it (bake it before filling it). This technique makes sure that it doesn't become soggy.

This versatile dish goes from brunch buffet to dinner table in a snap and is great with a leafy green salad. The flaky crust and custard filling make it a perfect vehicle for an array of mix-ins. Baking the crust before adding the filling, known as blind baking, ensures it won't get soggy.

Ingredients:

- 3/4 pound bacon, cooked and crumbled
- 3/4 cup heavy cream
- 1 tablespoon unsalted butter
- 1 cup shredded Gruyere cheese
- 1 homemade or store-bought single-crust pie dough
- 2 cups medium diced yellow onion
- 6 large eggs
- All-purpose flour, for rolling dough
- Coarse salt and ground pepper

Directions:

1. Preheat at 375^0 Use a rolling pin and roll out the dough into a 12-inch circle. Place it in a 9-inch pie plate, then fold the overhanging edges under and crimp the edges. Place parchment paper on top of the dough and add pie weight or dry beans to add some weight to the surface. Bake it until light golden for 20 minutes. Remove the parchment paper and weight and set aside.
2. In the meantime, melt butter in a skillet over medium flame. Add onion, pepper, and season with salt and cook for 8-10 minutes until light golden.
3. Whisk eggs and cream in a medium bowl. Add onion, cheese, bacon, and season it with ½ tsp salt and ¼ tsp pepper. Whisk it all to combine well.

4. Pour this into the baked crust and put it into the oven for another 40-45 minutes. Serve hot or at room temperature.

PEPPERONI SPINACH QUICHE

For a pool party, you need the ideal appetizer! A colorful Quiche is the best recipe to give your guests a treat. It looks amazing if you cut it into wedges and place it on an antipasto tray.

Ingredients:

- 1 tablespoon minced fresh parsley
- 1 tablespoon olive oil
- 1 tablespoon minced fresh basil or 1 teaspoon dried basil
- 1 large sweet red pepper, chopped
- 1 tube (about 8 ounces) refrigerated crescent rolls
- 1 garlic clove, minced
- 5 eggs, lightly beaten
- Dash pepper
- 1/4 cup sliced pepperoni, cut into strips
- 1/4 cup half-and-half cream
- 1/2 cup frozen chopped spinach, thawed and squeezed dry
- 1/2 cup shredded part-skim mozzarella cheese
- 2 tablespoons grated Parmesan cheese

Directions:

1. For this recipe, you must first separate the crest dough into 8 evenly cut triangles. Place them in an ungreased fluted tart pan that is 9-inch deep, and it must have a removable bottom with centrally placed points. Press it onto the bottom and then upside

down. This will form a sealed crust. Keep this aside for now.
2. Sauté the red pepper in some oil, but for this you need a small skillet. Add some garlic to it, and then cook it for 1 minute. Take it off the heat. Take another bowl and mix the other ingredients, and then add the pepper to it. Pour this into the crust.
3. Let this bake at 350^0 until the knife comes out clean or for 25-30 minutes. Before cutting it, let this stand for 5 minutes.
4. If you choose to freeze it, wrap it in foil or plastic wraps. To bake it, keep in the refrigerator overnight and let it thaw. The next day, preheat the oven at 350^0, unwrap the Quiche, and then bake. Keep a thermometer in the center and make sure it reads 165^0 while baking. This recipe serves 8 people.

POTATO CRUST QUICHE

Most people love potatoes and want it in every meal. Here's a new way of making Quiche and serving it with a salad. Everyone you serve this meal to, is sure to love it.

Ingredients:

CRUST:

- 1/2 teaspoon salt
- 1/2 cup chopped onion
- 1 cup all-purpose flour
- 1 egg, lightly beaten
- 4 cups coarsely shredded uncooked potatoes

FILLING:

- 1/2 teaspoon salt

- 1/2 cup chopped onion
- 1-1/2 cups shredded Colby cheese, divided
- 1 cup half-and-half cream
- 1-1/2 cups fresh broccoli florets
- 1-1/2 cups cubed fully cooked ham
- Paprika
- Dash ground nutmeg
- 3 egg, lightly beaten

Directions:

1. Combine the crust ingredients in a large bowl. Place it in a 10-inch well-greased deep-dish pie plate. Bake it for 20 minutes at 400^0.
2. Take it out from the oven and reduce the heat of the oven to 350^0. Add 1 cup of onions, broccoli, cheese, and ham to the crust. Whisk the eggs, cream, and nutmeg, salt. Pour this on the broccoli and sprinkle paprika over it.
3. Put it back in the oven to bake for 35-40 minutes or until the knife comes out clean. When ready, sprinkle the remaining cheese on top and let it stand for 5minutes before you serve. This recipe served 8 people.

BACON SWISS QUICHE RECIPE

This is a scrumptious recipe and ideal for breakfast and brunch. You can also serve it for dinner. Whenever you prefer having it, make sure you serve it with chilled grape clumps or any fresh fruit.

Ingredients:

- 1 tablespoon butter
- 1 sheet refrigerated pie pastry

- 1/8 teaspoon pepper
- 1/8 teaspoon salt
- 1/4 cup sliced green onions
- 1/4 cup unsweetened apple juice
- 1-1/2 cups heavy whipping cream
- 1 pound sliced bacon, cooked and crumbled
- 2 cups shredded Swiss cheese
- 6 eggs

Directions:

1. Preheat the oven to a temperature of 350^0. While it heats, line a 9-inch pie plate with the pastry. Trim the edges and flute them. Keep this aside for now.
2. In a small skillet, sauté the green onions in the butter until tender.
3. Whisk the eggs with the juice and cream. Then mix in the bacon, green onions, and pepper. Pour this combination into the pastry and sprinkle the cheese on top.
4. Put it in the oven and bake for 40-45 minutes or until the knife comes out clean when you insert it in the center. Do not cut it immediately; let it stand for at least 10 minutes.
5. If you choose to freeze it, wrap it in a plastic wrap or foil, and secure it before freezing. To bake it later, thaw it first by keeping it in the refrigerator overnight. Before baking, remove it from the refrigerator 30 minutes before baking. Make sure you preheat the oven at 350^0. Unwrap the Quiche, reheat the oven, place a thermometer in the center, and make sure it reads 165^0. This recipe serves 6 people.

CHEESY ZUCCHINI QUICHE

This Zucchini recipe is quick to prepare and storing in the freezer makes it an amazing quick snack option. All you need to do is refrigerate it overnight to thaw and put it into your oven to bake for 40 minutes.

Ingredients:

- 1/4 teaspoon pepper
- 1/2 teaspoon each dried basil and oregano
- 1/2 teaspoon each salt and garlic powder
- 1 large onion, thinly sliced
- 2 teaspoons prepared mustard
- 2 teaspoons dried parsley flakes
- 2 large eggs
- 2 cups part-skim shredded mozzarella cheese
- 3 tablespoons butter
- 4 cups thinly sliced zucchini
- Pastry for single-crust pie

Directions:

1. Preheat your oven at 400^0. Roll the pastry on a floured surface into a 1/8 inch thick circle. Place it in a 9-inch pie plate and flute the edges. Keep this in the refrigerator while preparing the other ingredients for the filling.
2. Heat the butter in a large skillet, at medium heat. Add onion and zucchini into the butter and still until it cooks and becomes tender. Drain the butter and let it cool slightly.
3. Whisk the eggs and add seasoning in a separate bowl. Add in the zucchini mixture and cheese and stir. Then, spread mustard over the pastry shell and add in the filling.

4. Bake for 35-40 minutes. Keep it on the lower rack of your oven and check using a knife if it has baked. Make sure the crust is golden brown. Cover the edges with foil during the last 15 minutes of baking if necessary to prevent over browning. Once baked, don't cut immediately. Let it stand for at least 10 minutes. This recipe serves 8 people.

Other option:

1. If you use pastry for 9-inch single-crust pie, to the 1 ¼ cups of all-purpose flour add ¼ tsp of salt. Add in the ½ cup of cold butter and gradually add 3-5 tbsp. of ice water. Mix it well until the dough forms firmly. Wrap it in plastic wrap and refrigerate for 1 hour.
2. Follow the steps for preparing the filling and putting it into the pastry and bake for 35-40 minutes or until the knife comes out clean when you insert it. Let it stand for at least 10 minutes before cutting. This pastry will serve 6 people.
3. Serve this dish with sour cream.

ASPARAGUS CUSTARD TART

This Quiche recipe is very rich and creamy. It has a puff pastry, cream, goat cheese, and Gruyere. However, it is a light meal! You can serve it with some fresh green salad to make a satisfying complete supper.

Ingredients:

- 2 ounces fresh goat cheese, crumbled into large pieces
- 1 tablespoon all-purpose flour, plus more for work surface
- 1 1/2 ounces Gruyere cheese, finely shredded
- 1 cup heavy cream

- 1 sheet frozen puff pastry (about 17.3-ounces), thawed
- Coarse salt
- 1 pound asparagus, trimmed, cut into 2-inch pieces, keep the stalks and tips separate
- 2 teaspoons extra-virgin olive oil
- 4 large eggs, room temperature

Directions:

1. Use the rolling pin to roll out the puff pastry into a 14-inch square. Flour the surface lightly, cut it into 13-inch circles using the paring knife. You can alternatively use a plate or bowl as a template. Transfer this into a round baking dish, or into a 5 ½ to 6 cup deep-dish pie plate. Prick all over using a fork. Freeze it until it is firm (for 30 minutes).
2. Preheat the oven at 350^0. Line the tart shell using a parchment. Fill it with dried beans to add weight to it. Place it on a baking sheet and bake for 40 minutes, until it turns golden. Return the crust to the oven, and bake it until the bottom turns golden brown and dry. This can take 5-10 minutes. Cool it on a wire rack.
3. Boil water in a medium pot, and add 2 tbsp. of salt to it. Put the asparagus stalks in the water and cook for 2 minutes, until it turns crisp-tender. Then, transfer the asparagus to a bowl filled with ice. Cool it, and then transfer it to a plate and pat it dry. Then add the asparagus tips into boiling water and cook it for 30 seconds. Drain off the water and place it in ice water. When cold, drain the water, and pat it dry again. Then toss it into a bowl with oil. Transfer the stalks to a blender, and add eggs with the flour, cream, and eggs. Add 1 ¼ tsp of salt and blend it into a puree that is very smooth.

4. Add custard into the crust. Sprinkle Gruyere and goat cheese and top it using the asparagus tips.
5. Bake it until the custard-filled edges puff up and turn golden brown. Check the center with a knife and bake it well. This may take 40 minutes. If necessary, tent it with foil to prevent excess browning.
6. Place it on a wire rack to let it cool for at least 15 minutes before serving.

HAM-AND-POTATO BAKE

This recipe is amazing and unique. It is crust-less! Imagine a crust-less Quiche that you can serve hot, cold or even at room temperature.

Ingredients:

- 10 ounces sugar-baked ham, thinly sliced
- 1/2 teaspoon ground pepper
- 1/2 cup grated cheddar cheese
- 1 package (about 10 ounces) frozen broccoli, thawed and squeezed dry with paper towels
- 1 1/2 cups heavy cream
- 2 teaspoons coarse salt
- 2 baking potatoes (1 1/4 pounds), peeled
- 6 large eggs
- Butter, for pan

Directions:

1. Let the oven preheat at 350^0. Use a 9-inch cake pan that is at least 2 inch deep and line the bottom with parchment paper.
2. Whisk the eggs with the cream in a large bowl.

3. Slice the potatoes into thin slices that are less than ¼ inch thick. Add these to the egg and cream mixture.
4. Take out half of the slices of potatoes out ad arrange them in the pan. Add a layer of ham, cheese, broccoli, and the remaining half of the potatoes in the pan. Pour the egg mixture on top to cover the dough and press down firmly to submerge the sliced potatoes.
5. Cover it with foil and bake until the potatoes become tender. This can take 1 hour. Then, uncover it and continue baking it until it turns golden for 30-45 minutes. Let it set.

Leave it for 15-20 minutes in the pan, and then run the knife around to release the edges and invert it onto a plate. Peel off the parchment, and turn it over again to make the top side up. Slice it using a toothed or serrated knife and serve.

SWISS CHARD, MUSHROOM, AND WHITE-CHEDDAR QUICHE

For a rich and creamy Quiche that is ideal for the family, this recipe will be the best. It combines vegetables, cheese, and custard, with a flaky shell, which is the perfect for a brunch. You just have to sauté the pastry and prepare the pastry a night before.

Ingredients:

THE CRUST INGREDIENTS

- 1/4 cup plus 3 tablespoons ice water
- 1 large egg, plus 1 large egg yolk
- 2 sticks unsalted butter, cut into small pieces and frozen until firm
- 2 2/3 cups all-purpose flour, more for surface
- Vegetable oil cooking spray
- Coarse salt

THE FILLING INGREDIENTS

- 1 pound cremini mushrooms, thinly sliced
- 1 bunch Swiss chard (about 12 ounces), stems and ribs removed, washed and coarsely chopped (about 8 cups)
- 2 large garlic cloves, minced
- 2 1/2 cups shredded sharp white cheddar (6 1/2 ounces)
- 3 tablespoons unsalted butter
- 3 1/4 cups half-and-half
- 9 large eggs
- Coarse salt and freshly ground pepper

Directions:

1. To make the crust, Mix the butter with the flour, add 1 tsp salt, and use the food processor to mix it until it looks like a coarse batter with large pieces. Whisk the eggs and yolk with water. Pulse the flour mixture and drizzle the egg mix into it until the dough forms. Put the dough into the plastic wrap, and make it into a rectangle and wrap it safely. Refrigerate it for an hour, until firm.
2. On a floured surface, roll the dough into a rectangle shape measuring 14 x 12 inches. Refrigerate it for 15 minutes to make it firm. Coat the rimmed baking sheet with some cooking spray. Put the dough in the sheet and fold the excess underneath, and pinch it to make the crust come ½ inch above the rim. Freeze it until firm for 30 minutes.
3. Let the oven preheat at 375^0 and place one rack on the lower third section and the other rack in the middle. You must line the dough with the parchment and flush it leaving 2-inch overhang on all the sides.

Fold the parchment to cover the edges of the crust. Add dried beans on top to add pie-weight. Bake it on the lower rack. Rotate the tray halfway into 40 minutes. Remove the pie weight and parchment. Then bake it until it turns crisp and golden brown. This can take 15-17 minutes. Let it cool by placing it on a wire rack.

4. Reduce the temperature of the oven to 325^0 and prepare the filling in the meantime. Heat 2 tbsp. of butter in a skillet over medium flame. Cook the mushrooms for 8 minutes until tender (you may have to adjust the heat). Season it with ½ tsp salt, pepper to taste, and transfer it to a bowl.
5. Allow the skillet to cool down. Add the remaining tbsp. of butter. Cook the garlic on low heat and stir it for 1 minute until it become fragrant. Stir while adding the chard, and then season it with ½ tsp salt and pepper to taste. Cook it for 6 minutes and stir occasionally until it becomes tender. Increase the heat and cook it until the liquid evaporates then toss in the chard and mushrooms. Allow it to cool to room temperature.
6. Whisk the half-and-half with the eggs, and add 2 tsps. of salt. Sprinkle the 1 ¼ cups of cheese on the tart crust. Put the mushroom-chard over this layer and sprinkle the remaining cheese over it. Gradually and evenly, spread the custard over the cheese and vegetable layers. Do not let it become more than ¼ inch from the top of the crust. Discard the excess. To bake it, place it on the middle rack, rotate it halfway into the 35-40 minutes baking. Let the Quiche stand on the wire rack for at least 15 minutes before cutting it into squares. Serve it immediately.

This recipe tastes amazing with sautéed garlic cloves, filled with other mouthwatering caramelized ingredients.

Ingredients:

- 3/4 tablespoon sugar
- 3/4 teaspoon fine sea salt
- 1 teaspoon balsamic vinegar
- 1 tablespoon olive oil
- 1 teaspoon chopped fresh rosemary
- 1 teaspoon chopped fresh thyme, plus 3 sprigs for garnish
- 2 large eggs
- 3 medium heads of garlic, cloves separated and peeled
- 4 1/2 ounces soft, creamy goat cheese, such as chevre
- 4 1/2 ounces hard, mature goat cheese, such as goat gouda
- 6 1/2 tablespoons heavy cream
- 6 1/2 tablespoons crème fraiche
- 13 ounces puff pastry, defrosted if frozen
- Freshly ground black pepper

Directions:

1. Preheat the oven at 350^0.
2. Roll the puff pastry dough into a 16-inch circle. Fit the puff pastry into an 11 x 1 ½ inch fluted round pan, which has a removable bottom. Place the parchment paper around the top and add weight or dry beans.
3. Place it in the refrigerator for 20 minutes or until it chills.
4. Put the tart shell in the preheated oven and bake it for 20 minutes. Remove the weights and paper, and let it bake until golden. This may take 5-10 minutes.

Remove it from the oven and keep it aside while you work on the filling.

5. Put the garlic cloves into a saucepan with enough boiling water. Let it simmer over medium heat for 3 minutes. Drain the water and put the cloves in the saucepan. Add olive oil, and heat it to cook the cloves. Stir occasionally until the cloves look fried (for 2 minutes). Add 1 tsp vinegar and 1 cup of water and let it simmer for an additional 10 minutes. Add chopped thyme, rosemary, ¼ tsp salt, and sugar and let it simmer until the water evaporates (for 10 minutes) and the garlic coats in the dark caramelized syrup. Remove it from the flame and keep it aside.
6. Break the goat cheese into pieces and scatter it in the tart shell. Put the garlic cloves and the syrup over the cheese.
7. Whisk the cream, eggs, crème fraiche, and ½ tsp salt and pepper in a large glass-measuring cup. Pour this mixture over the garlic filling and cheese, but let them be visible.
8. Put the tart in the oven and bake until the filling sets and turns golden brown. Take it out and cool before you remove it from the tart pan. You can trim it if necessary, and garnish it with thyme sprigs before serving.

ASPARAGUS, LEEK, AND GRUYERE QUICHE

Nothing beats the amazing taste of Gruyere, the Swiss cheese that has been famous for adding a nutty flavor to every recipe. This cheese works amazingly with egg and vegetables.

Ingredients:

- 1 tablespoon butter

- 1 cup shredded Gruyere cheese
- 1 leek (white and light green parts only), halved and thinly sliced, then well washed
- 1 bunch (about 1 pound) asparagus, tough ends removed, thinly sliced on the diagonal
- 1 1/4 cups half-and-half
- 4 large eggs
- Ground nutmeg
- Coarse salt and ground pepper
- Our Favorite Pie Crust, fitted into a 9-inch pie plate, well chilled

Directions:

1. In a preheated oven at 350^0, place the rack at the lowest position. Melt the butter in a large skillet over medium flame. Toss in the asparagus and leek, season it with pepper and salt, and stir it at intervals until asparagus turns crisp and tender. This takes 6-8 minutes. Then let it cool.
2. Whisk the eggs together with 1 ¼-cup half-and-half, nutmeg (a pinch), teaspoon full pepper, and ½ tsp salt. Put the piecrust on the baking sheet, sprinkle the cheese, and top it with the asparagus mixture. Pour the egg mixture over this.
3. Bake it for 50-60 minutes until the Quiche sets. Rotate the sheet halfway through. After baking, let it stand aside for 15 minutes before serving.

SAUSAGE-POTATO QUICHE

This recipe needs just an hour to prepare, so if you want to impress your guests with a snappy snack, then serve this Sausage-Potato Quiche. If you love green leafy salads, then you can combine it with this recipe when serving. Because you have to use the blind-baking technique, be sure that the Quiche won't turn soggy.

This versatile dish goes from brunch buffet to dinner table in a snap and is great with a leafy green salad. Baking the crust before adding the filling, known as blind baking, ensures it won't get soggy.

Ingredients:

- 3/4 cup heavy cream
- 3/4 pound russet potato, cubed and steamed until tender
- 1 tablespoon unsalted butter
- 1 cup finely grated Parmesan
- 1 homemade or store-bought single-crust pie dough
- 2 cups crumbled cooked spicy Italian sausage
- Coarse salt and ground pepper
- 6 large eggs
- All-purpose flour, for rolling

Directions:

1. You must preheat the oven at 350^0. While it heats, roll the dough using a rolling pin and floured surface into a 12-inch circle. Place it into a 9-inch pie plate, fold the overhang underneath, and crimp the edge. Use parchment and dried beans to add weight on the dough. Then bake it until light golden for 20 minutes.
2. In the meantime, melt butter in a large skillet over medium flame. Add the sausages, pepper, and salt seasoning and let it cook until it turns light golden. This should take 8-10 minutes.
3. Whisk the eggs with cream in another bowl. Add sausages, potatoes, and cheese and season it with ¼ tsp pepper and ½ tsp salt. Whisk thoroughly, add to

the crust, and bake for 40-45 minutes it until the center bakes through well. Serve it while warm or cool it to room temperature.

THANK YOU

If you have truly found value in my publication please take a minute and rate my book, I'd be eternally grateful if you left a review. As an independent author I rely on reviews for my livelihood and it gives me great pleasure to see my work is appreciated.

Printed in Great Britain
by Amazon